WITHDRAWN

WHAT I BELIEVE

Kids Talk about Faith

by Debbie Holsclaw Birdseye and Tom Birdseye

photographs by Robert Crum

Holiday House/New York

For our parents,
Buster and Jerry Holsclaw,
and Irving and Mary Hughes Birdseye
D.H.B. & T.B.

To my sisters,
Julie and Barbara
R.C.

Text copyright © 1996 by Debbie Holsclaw Birdseye and Tom Birdseye
Photographs copyright © 1996 by Robert Crum
ALL RIGHTS RESERVED
Printed in the United States of America
FIRST EDITION

Library of Congress Cataloging-in-Publication Data
Birdseye, Debbie Holsclaw.
What I believe: kids talk about faith / by Debbie Holsclaw
Birdseye and Tom Birdseye; photographs by Robert Crum.
p. cm.
Includes bibliographical references.
Summary: Six children of different religious backgrounds tell
about their faith and what it means to them.
ISBN 0-8234-1268-7 (alk. paper)
1. Religions—Juvenile literature. [1. Religions.]
I. Birdseye, Tom. II. Crum, Robert, ill. III. Title.
BL92.B57   1996   96-11240   CIP   AC
200'.83—dc20

Introduction

This is a book about religion, but not religion on a grand scale. You will find no long, detailed passages of religious history here. Nor will you find any attempt to present and explain the wide variety of religious beliefs and rituals from around the world.

Instead, this book is an opportunity for you to go beyond the *what, when, where,* and *why* of religion and arrive at a very individual *who.* It is a chance to meet—up close and personal—six kids from six different religious backgrounds.

Janani, Min, Carmel, Alex, Aly, and Kaila. This book is about what they believe.

Authors' Note

In the spring of 1995, a group of children in Corvallis, Oregon, put together a list of questions that asked adults about their religious beliefs. The answers they gathered were very interesting, but we found ourselves more curious about how kids would respond to the same sort of questions, especially kids from different religious backgrounds. So we decided to put together a questionnaire of our own and do a little asking, too.

But, like most things in life, it wasn't quite that simple. There are hundreds, if not thousands, of religious traditions in the world, each with its own set of firmly held beliefs and rituals. (For example, just within the United States there are more than two hundred active Christian denominations.) We couldn't possibly include a child from each sect or subsect of every religion in the world. How could we choose? Who should we ask?

After a lot of thought (and worry about who might feel left out), we finally narrowed the choices down to six: Hinduism, Buddhism, Judaism, Christianity, Islam, and Native American. We then went looking for six kids, understanding that even though we were seeking diverse views, we weren't expecting them to speak for their religions as a whole, or even for the particular sect or subsect to which they belong. That was not the point. The point was to explore what kids as *individuals* believe, and how those beliefs influence their day-to-day lives.

Despite what some people think—that today's youth are only interested in video games, rock music, TV, and food—finding kids who had given a lot of thought to their faith and were willing to talk about it turned out to be quite easy. The world, it seems, is brimming with them.

What we present here are their words, full of eagerness, sincerity, and hope.

Debbie Holsclaw Birdseye and Tom Birdseye
CORVALLIS, OREGON
JANUARY 1996

Janani

I am twelve years old and go to middle school. I play the violin and piano and like to read and write, ride my bike, and go for walks. I like math, too. It's a hobby of mine.

I am a Hindu. Some people think that in Hinduism we have a lot of separate gods, but we don't. To me, God means one superior being who takes many different forms that symbolize many different things.

There are gods that represent the forces of nature, like wind and rain. We have gods that represent the animal kingdom. There are gods that symbolize love, knowledge, and prosperity. There is a god with an elephant's head, who removes all obstacles. There's a monkey god, too. And God takes on ten different incarnations just to wipe out evil.

God has a male half and an equally powerful female half. Neither one can survive without the other. I think *It* when I'm talking about God, instead of *He* or *She*. That's comforting to me, because it's equal.

In Hinduism, we have many festivals and ceremonies that help me to understand how all the aspects of God tie together. They also help me to sort out all the beliefs, and how those beliefs apply to me. My parents and grandparents have given me a lot of ideas about how to think about God.

I believe that God is everywhere and nowhere, because the whole universe

In addition to playing the piano, Janani is an exceptional violinist.

is contained inside of God, and God is in the whole universe. God is in each one of us and knows everything that we are doing. So God sees, feels, and hears all that I do and knows everything about me.

To get close to God, or to communicate with It, some people do yoga meditation. That's where you just sit for ten or fifteen minutes and remove all thoughts from your mind. You are supposed to be practically unconsciousness sitting up. This helps you to relax and entirely concentrate on God. I've tried to do it, but yoga doesn't work for me. It's very difficult. I can't stop *thinking* about things. I have managed to meditate while reciting prayers, though.

I have respect for God. I say prayers when I'm thankful for things, and before I go to sleep. I pray whenever I want God to help me get through something or do well on a test. I don't say, "God, if you'll do *this*, then I'll do *that*." Because that would be bribing God.

I don't think that God works for anybody if you don't believe in It. If you just say, "God, please remove all my obstacles," without being sincere, God's not going to do anything. You have to really believe that you can surmount those obstacles. God will make you better at what you do only if you *work* at it.

In the Hindu religion, we believe in reincarnation and a concept called *karma.* Everybody is held responsible for their actions, or *karmas.* In their next life they are rewarded or punished for their deeds. So in the end, you never get away with anything bad. I think I was in somebody else's body before, or in something's form, although I haven't the slightest idea what. When I die, my soul will be born in another form, which will pay for my sins in this life.

I don't think God is offended by any mistakes that I might make, as long as I repent for them. Something that would be offensive to God, though, would be praying to It and expressing devotion to It without having any real devotion. God expects me to be honest with It.

In Hinduism, yoga meditation is used as a means to better communicate with God.

I don't believe God ever begins, and I don't think God ever ends. To say that would be like putting a date on God. I believe that God is just infinite in both directions. I like to think of it that way because it's very comforting. God is always there to take care of me. To put it another way, then I know that God won't run out of fuel.

That's my picture of my religion. I understand that other religions have different ideas about what happens. I respect their pictures, too.

Janani, her mother, and her grandparents in traditional East Indian dress.

Min

I was born in Thailand but moved to Australia when I was five. I started learning English there. Then, when I was ten, I moved to the United States. I'm twelve now and go to middle school. I have a little brother who is in kindergarten. On the weekends I like to play Super Nintendo or draw people. I like to be with my friends, too.

I'm Buddhist, and I do believe in it very much. In Buddhism we believe that we are rotating around. People die, people come back, people die, people come back. That's called reincarnation. We also believe that if you do good things, good things come back to you. If you don't punch people and don't do mean things to them, then they won't do mean things to you. But if you do bad things, then bad will follow you.

Some people do very bad things in their lives, and then they have to be born back into horrible lives. Like if you killed somebody, or if you pushed somebody off a building, then in your next life you might be pushed off a building, too.

After a lot of lifetimes, if you do really good, if you are perfect, then you won't be born again; you are sort of like immortal. Buddha was born a long time ago as a prince, and he started to learn. He had a lot of lives that were perfect. He became enlightened. Enlightenment is the truth, like you finally find the truth in yourself.

Much of Min's free time is spent with his friends.

I wear a necklace of Buddha, and I try to do like Buddha said—be a good person, follow the rules of Buddhism, and walk the middle path. The middle path means walk in peace, don't talk to yourself too much. So, if I want to do something, I don't work so hard that I never get any sleep. For example, if I studied every day, then I'd be too tired and wouldn't do well on a test. I'd fail. If I go the middle way—not too much hard work, but not too much relaxing, either—then I will probably get my training, and I will get an A.

Min wears a Buddha necklace similar to these as a reminder of his faith.

Every time I go to bed, I say a prayer. I put my hands together three times, I bow, and I pray for my parents and my family and to the Buddha. I say a prayer in the morning and sometimes at school, too. That way I feel like Buddha is with me, so I should do good. Prayer is like a step to meditation. It's the first step, the basic step.

In meditation you go and you sit down, and you close your eyes. You breathe in, breathe out. It's good for your lungs and your health. There are no words. You don't think anything. You relax and make your mind calm.

I meditate every day, if I have time, for about an hour. I meditate with my mom and my dad.

I'm teaching my brother to meditate. I'm teaching him about our religion, and how to pray. My mom and dad teach him, too, but I teach him the most.

On religious days, like the days the Buddha was born and died, we go to a temple. And on my birthday, too. I go to the monks and give them food, and they pray for me. They pour holy water on me that can make me good and take away evil. I went to a monk once who gave me a bracelet that he had put in the holy water. He called it the string of hope, and it protects me.

Min helps his parents teach his younger brother, Phun, about their religion.

My religion says that if I am a monk for about two months, then my mom and dad will go up to Heaven. It would be good for me to be a monk, for the happiness of my parents. They would cut off all my hair, and I would wear a yellow robe. I would start learning more prayers, and about religion, and to be calm, and to get more beliefs. So I will do that someday. It will be the experience of a lifetime.

Since I've been in other countries, I've learned how other people believe. But I keep my own religion. I believe in the Buddha. I think he's real. Buddhism helps me keep my life straight.

Carmel

I'm the youngest of three sisters. I like drama and had the lead part in the play at middle school. I was Alice in *Alice in Wonderland*. I baby-sit a lot and teach first-grade kids the Hebrew alphabet at the synagogue. I like to spend time with my friends. We talk on the phone a lot.

I had my bat mitzvah just after I turned thirteen. The bat mitzvah is an initiation ceremony. It means that you are now a responsible part of the Jewish community. To get ready for the bat mitzvah I did a lot of studying of the Torah. The Torah is like the Jewish Bible, only it's on a scroll. It's the basis of Jewish beliefs.

I wore my tallit, or prayer shawl, at the bat mitzvah. I also wore a head covering called a *kippah* that helped me to remain serious and think about why I was there. You are supposed to look at the fringes on the bottom of the shawl and remember all the commandments and the words from the Torah.

My rabbi said that when the Torah was first written, the same number of letters were in it as the number of Jews. So when you come up to your bat mitzvah, it's like finding your letter.

On Friday night we celebrate the beginning of Shabbat. Shabbat is the Jewish day of rest and worship. It's from Friday at sundown to the time on Saturday night when you can see three stars.

Carmel plays the part of Alice in her school production of Alice in Wonderland.

It's a tradition in my family that my mom will light the candles and say the prayers over them. My dad says the prayers over the wine or the grape juice. Then one of my sisters or me will say the prayers over the challah bread. We say them in Hebrew, not English. In more Orthodox families they would say prayers like that every day at every meal. There's such a wide range of beliefs in Judaism.

I pray at the synagogue, too. We go there for Friday night and Saturday morning services. There is a prayer you pray as a group, and it's in Hebrew. We say it two times. The first time is silent, and then we repeat it out loud. When I pray silently I can pray for whatever I want. I think that means a little more.

I might pray when I'm trying to do my best at things, and trying to make good judgments and do things that I think would be healthy for me. I guess that's sort of what God would like.

I don't think of God as a person, you know, with facial features or whatever. In Hebrew there's a masculine and feminine for each word, and *God* is written

An active member of her synagogue, Carmel teaches the Hebrew alphabet to a class of first-graders.

in the Torah in the masculine form. But you are taught, and I believe, that really God is not a male or a female.

God is pretty old. In the beginning God created all life, the first people, and the earth, and everything. So God was here first.

I believe that God is here to help but not tell you what to do. And so, in the Torah, God will say things and then leave it up to you to decide what they mean.

There are things that are real clear, though, against the commandments. It says in the Torah that man was created in God's image. So it's against Jewish law to commit suicide, because life is one of the most holy things. It would be like killing God if you killed yourself. Anything that would harm me, like drugs, that would not be good, either. I don't want to offend God.

But God is just and doesn't punish people. God just wants me to be the best, most educated person that I can be. So it's important to me to study hard and do the best I can.

Lots of things have happened to the Jews, like the Holocaust or the burning of the Temple a long time ago. A lot of people say, "Where is God?" But I believe what the rabbis say: God is with His people. When the Jews were forced to leave the Temple, God went with them. God is where His people are, and where people believe in Him. God is everywhere, all of the time, and is always listening.

Judaism is who I am. It's shaped my life. It affects everything I do. It's nice to have something to believe in, you know. When you think that there is a higher power, it seems like you're not alone.

Carmel's parents maintain many Jewish traditions in their household.

Alex

I'm thirteen years old and live with my parents. During the school year I spend most of my time on homework and big projects. But I like to draw all sorts of things. I'm in the Boy Scouts. We have all kinds of camp-outs and community service events.

At church, I'm in the youth group. We do fun things, like dinners together. We have events such as shopping for needy people, too.

It was my decision to become a Christian. That's more meaningful to me, I think, because I can say I chose that and hold myself to it. I was baptized into the church by being dunked in water. It was cold, very cold. They had us in some sort of gownlike robe. I was about nine or ten at the time.

In my religion we believe that Jesus is the gift that God gave us. That's why we give gifts at Christmas time. Jesus taught with words and actions. He was willing to give His life for a greater purpose—to relieve our sins, so we're forgiven for whatever we do. The little white lie, or something big, we don't have to bear that burden.

Some people would say that God is this bearded old man leaning on his cane. Some people think that God is inside them, like a feeling. I've never seen God. I can't really say where He is, like up on a mountain. It's possible that I've heard Him, but that might just be my own thoughts.

When he isn't doing homework, Alex enjoys drawing.

I think God is probably very, very old, ancient. Maybe He's older than the universe. And He's out around me everywhere, without limits, not in a particular place.

I don't take the Bible literally. I don't think the earth was actually created in six days. I think it's more imagery and symbolic. But I believe in God because there are some things that cannot be rationally explained. We're here and the world is here. How did that happen?

God is there, like a friend I haven't met. He understands and possibly intervenes. He helps me in my daily life, gives me confidence when I need it, and insight into some things.

Some people think that God still works miracles. I believe maybe, occasionally. But if I pray for getting an A on this test and I get an A, is that really

The congregation of Alex's church stands to sing a hymn.

God, or is it me? I've prayed for some things that haven't happened. So I'm not sure that there's direct intervention, but sometimes there are moments when I feel close to God.

Usually I thank God for everything that's happened this week. Sometimes I ask for help on something. Through a story I heard at church, I learned a lesson about asking for things. There was this burning fire. And this guy kneels down and says, "God, could you put out the fire for me?" And of course the guy is just standing there, and the fire is burning. Why doesn't he grab a bucket? The only thing God can do is help. He can't do it for him. So, I ask Him for help on things instead of saying, "Please do this for me. Please do that for me."

God expects me to live by the Commandments. They are guidelines of how you should be, what you should shoot for. To me they mean to be respectful of other people and their rights. Probably the worst thing that I could do would be to lie to my parents. I think that would tick God off.

The closest person that I've known that lives in a godly way was probably my grandpa. He died a couple of years ago. He was very kind to people, and generous and wise, and he shared what he knew. I try to be like that and to have faith.

I think that faith is an essential part of religion. It's trust in what you believe. That's what gets you through. Being a Christian has taught me to be more caring and kind. I like to think I'm a nicer person because of it.

Alex's parents supported his decision to be baptized into the church.

Aly

My parents are from Egypt, but I was born in California twelve years ago. I have one younger brother and sister, and two sisters who are older than me.

My favorite sport is basketball. I play a lot. I used to spend my money on sports cards, but not so much anymore. I like to sit around with my friends from middle school, too.

I am a Muslim, and it means everything to me. It's my life. I believe that there is only one God, who is gracious and most merciful, and that Prophet Muhammad is the last messenger of God. God has ninety-nine names. We used to have all ninety-nine of them on a paper, and my mom would recite them to us in Arabic. God's most common name is Allah.

Arabic is the language of Islam. We have Arabic school every Sunday. My mom is our teacher. I got most of my information from my mom and my dad. My mom is an important part of the family. She keeps herself covered around men, even her face with a scarf, except at home with our family. That's what it says in the Quran. My dad supports the family, and he sits down with us and helps us read the Quran with our mom.

The Quran is God's word. If you read one verse of the Quran you think, "No person could have made this up."

This is kind of embarrassing, but when I was a little kid I used to hug the

Aly is a big basketball fan, and a player in his own right.

air, because I thought that God was everywhere. Now I know that I can't see or hug God, but He is still there. I believe in Him. When I pray to God I face the Kaaba, which is a mosque in Saudi Arabia. A mosque is the house of God. I touch my forehead and nose to the ground. That's the way that Prophet Muhammad told us how to pray, kneeling before God.

There are five prayers during the day. *Fajr* is the first one. It starts before the sun comes up. Then there's *duhar*, which starts about noon. And then *asr*, which is from 2 P.M. to 4 P.M. *Maghrib* is at sundown. *Isha* is the final prayer. I pray verses from the Quran. I've memorized a lot of the Quran.

Every day, all the five prayers are held at the mosque. On Friday a person gives a speech, and then we pray. If I pray at the mosque, I get twice the good deeds. I can pray at my house, too. I don't get as many good deeds, but I still get some.

In Islam, we believe there are good deeds and bad deeds. The good deeds are like whenever I pray or give to charity, or if I help any person, like an old woman crossing the street. If I smile at someone, that's a good deed, too.

Bad deeds are things that God wouldn't like. If I eat pork or drink alcohol, those are bad deeds. If I do bad things to anybody, like hit somebody or say a cussword, then I get a bad deed.

God expects me to fast during the sacred month of Ramadan. Ramadan is twenty-nine or thirty days, depending on the lunar calendar, and comes eleven days earlier each year, so it moves over time. In the morning during Ramadan, before the sun comes up, I eat and drink a lot so I won't be thirsty. Then when

Muslims must pray five times daily facing the Kaaba, a mosque in Saudi Arabia.

the sunlight comes I can't eat anymore until sundown. We say lots of verses from the Quran during Ramadan.

I believe that God will forgive me for just about anything, except if I worship anything other than Allah or worship someone as equal to Allah. He is the one who created me and sent me to earth. And if he could do all that, and bring me back, then he can do anything he wants.

We are not supposed to ask how God knows everything or how He originated. But I know that God has been around from time and beyond. God sees from Adam to the last person on earth. Time doesn't exist for God. God is the greatest of all.

I am dedicated to being a Muslim and following Islam. It keeps me away from bad things and helps me stay clean. It shows me the right path.

Aly with his father, brother, and three sisters who cover themselves according to Muslim tradition.

Kaila

I'm thirteen years old, and I live with my mom and my dad and my little brother. I have two cats and lots of good friends in middle school that I've known since kindergarten. We've been in the same class for all of those years.

I like to do creative things with my hands, like draw people and faces. I like debate, too, where you stand up and prove a point.

My religion is Native American, and it's my way of seeing what life is. It gives me perspective.

Our church is a sweat lodge. It's a small place made of willow branches with blankets over it. It's dark inside. Someone gets rocks out of the fire and puts them in the middle of the sweat lodge. Then people get in and sit in a circle around the hot rocks. The water thrower pours water on the rocks, which makes steam. So it's really hot in there, and you sweat.

I believe that the sweat lodge is like a mother's womb. Going in there is kind of like taking off all your old regrets and renewing yourself. It's like if you wake up in the morning with all that gunk in your mouth, and then you brush your teeth, and your mouth feels nice and clean.

I pray in the sweat lodge for my family, and for food to eat, and for healing, and for help in my life. It depends. And then when I come out, it's like being reborn, and I feel new again. It's really neat. It gives me a way to be in connection with the Creator.

Kaila holds a picture she has drawn of Chief Joseph, the great leader of the Nez Perce.

We have powwows with drumming and singing. Everyone dresses up and dances in a big circle. We carry sacred symbols, like the eagle feather. If you drop one it is really, really bad. But mainly the powwow is a celebration.

The sun dance is different. It's a sacred ceremony. The day before it starts, they cut down a tree and people put prayer ties on it. Then they stand the tree up in the center of the arbor.

When the sun dancers walk into the arbor the next day at sunrise, the sun flows over them. They have their feather fans, and the eagle-bone whistle to blow, and sage. Some of them dance for four days without eating or drinking anything. The men pierce their backs and drag buffalo skulls around. They do that as sacrifice, a show of faith in life, like a woman giving birth.

Being at a sun dance is like my regular self kind of peeling away. The desert is beautiful, and there are wild horses that run in the mountains. It's very powerful and spiritual. I feel safe, like the Creator is watching me.

I know that the Creator exists because . . . well, how else did the world and all of us get here? *Something* had to create it.

The Creator is a higher power and is everywhere and inside of everything. I can't see It, or hear It, or touch It. (I don't really want to say *he* or *she*. I don't think the Creator has a race or age or anything, either.) It's just there and always has been.

Kaila prays at a shrine during a sweat lodge ceremony.

I think the Creator knows my life and everything that's going to happen. I try not to do bad things. Sometimes I make mistakes, though. But I don't believe that if I do, I'll go to Hell. Because mistakes are a part of life. And I'm not going to be sent to Hell for living. I can't go back to the past and change my actions, but I may be able to do good actions and change the way people think about me.

I believe that life is an ongoing thing. It's a blessing. You live and you learn, you make mistakes, and you learn some more. And so you become wise over a lifetime, and you die. It may be hard to get through the parting with someone, but you're not apart forever. Mother Earth has been around for a long time. It's like one big life. So you just come back, and you learn even more. And you keep on getting wiser and wiser. Medicine men are like that. They've been around for a long time.

I think my religion helps me to be a good person. It helps me to respect Mother Earth and nature, and my elders, and my family—which is really important to me. It also helps me to accept people for who they are are. It's what I believe.

Both Kaila's father, who is Klamath, and her mother, who is not Native American, participate in traditional ceremonies.

Acknowledgements

Many people helped bring this book into being. First and foremost are Janani, Min, Carmel, Alex, Aly, Kaila, and all of their families. To be welcomed into their lives with such openness and honesty was an honor.

The following people also lent a hand in many different ways: Jill McAllister, Art Wilmot, Michael Plotnick, John Evans, Khahid Khan, Barbara Grant, Sally Arico, Linda Gallen, Jayashree Deshmukl, Abby Kennedy, Bahaa Wanly, Ann Manheimer, the staff of the Corvallis-Benton County (Oregon) Public Library, Jean Naggar, Margery Cuyler, and Regina Griffin.

To all of you, and to any others we may have inadvertently left out, a great big THANK YOU!

Debbie Holsclaw Birdseye
Tom Birdseye
Robert Crum

Further Reading

BROWN, STEPHEN F. *Christianity*. New York: Facts on File, 1991.

GORDON, MATTHEW S. *Islam*. New York: Facts on File, 1991.

HEWITT, CATHERINE. *Buddhism*. New York: Thomson Learning, 1995.

KADODWALA, DILIP. *Hinduism*. New York: Thomson Learning, 1996.

KNIGHT, KHADIJAN. *Islam*. New York: Thomson Learning, 1996.

LOGAN, JOHN. *Christianity*. New York: Thomson Learning, 1996.

MORRISON, MARTHA & BROWN, STEPHEN F. *Judaism*. New York: Facts on File, 1991.

SHERROW, VICTORIA. *Spiritual Life* (Native American Culture). Vero Beach, Florida: Rourke Publications, 1994.

SITA, LISA. *Worlds of Belief: Religion and Spirituality*. Woodbridge, Connecticut: Blackbirch Press, 1996.

WANGU, MADHU BAZAZ. *Buddhism*. New York: Facts on File, 1993.

WANGU, MADHU BAZAZ. *Hinduism*. New York: Facts on File, 1991.

WILSON, JAMES. *Native Americans* (Threatened Cultures). New York: Thomson Learning, 1994.

WOOD, ANGELA. *Judaism*. New York: Thomson Learning, 1995.